Angels and Answers

Angels and Answers

...

Artie Hoffman

For a private psychic/medium reading in person, over the phone or Skype, or to book a party, event or public speaking. Contact information below.

732-778-7173 or 877-Angel-02

Artiehoffman.com

Artiehoffman@gmail.com

Facebook Angels and Answers

ISBN: 0692991565
ISBN 13: 9780692991565

This book is filled with so much positive loving energy. It's filled with lots of inspirational messages and gorgeous pictures of saints, angels, and spiritual birds. Through prayer and meditation this book has been blessed by Angels, Saints, and The Holy Spirit and now by you taking ownership of this book filled with love. You have now just been blessed yourself, Amen.

"The Voice for the Unheard"
                    Artie Hoffman

Acknowledgments

■ ■ ■

HUMBLY I WOULD LIKE TO thank God for sending all the Angels that have come to me in my lifetime, and for giving me the ability to understand the wisdom that has been graced upon me.

Thank you God for loving me, nurturing my heart and soul, and for giving me the happiness and confidence to serve the public while serving you. I graciously accept all your blessings, miracles, and gifts you wish to share with me as I share your love and wisdom with others.

They say behind every successful man there's a woman or partner that gives you the support you need to be the best you can be. No one person can do it all by themselves.

They say it takes years to be an overnight success, and in my case, that's definitely true. If it wasn't for my partner and the love of my life Alison putting the fire under my ass, this book with all these beautiful messages that I wrote many years ago would still be on the shelf.

And a great thanks to my wonderful friend and Personal Assistant Ilona Gottwald for keeping my life organized and balanced in many ways.

Just know Angels don't just come to us only in spirit form, they also show up as people. People Angels come to you in your life for many countless reasons, during your best times and especially during your most challenging times. God sends you these beautiful spirits when you need them the most.

So, thank you God for bringing me all the Angel friends and family members into my life, for supporting me, and for bringing me and showing me the lessons I need to know in this lifetime.

Thank you, God, for blessing me with my wonderful daughter Rebecca.
I'd like to thank my mother Edith Hoffman for loving me unconditionally and giving me the support and confidence that helped me stay strong, when at times I wanted to give up. Her laughter, sense of humor, and words of wisdom helped me get through some rough times in my life and see life's situations through a healthy perspective. My mom would always say to me, "It's OK to get older, just don't get old."
I would like to thank Krystal Mannering for creating my book cover.
To Dawn Anderson, thank you for sharing the beautiful picture titled, "Sky of Angels," that you took when we drove to Lake George, NY – the picture is in the section titled, "It's Me Mom."
Thank you to all the talented artists who drew and created the illustrations of all the Angels featured within these pages: Christine Little, Krystal Mannering, Eleni Toto, Gregory Lawler, and Anthony Noonan.
Last, but not least, I would like to thank the thousands of people that I have read for in the past and the wonderful people that contact me daily for messages, hope, and inspiration.

May God bless all of you!

Forward

■ ■ ■

YOU WILL FIND THIS BOOK will explain certain realities of life through the eyes of love and spirituality. These messages you are about to read are words that will elegantly but simply relate to your feelings and emotions. You will feel like you are being understood on a very deep level.

These beautiful thoughts and messages were brought to me randomly throughout the days and evenings as I was just going about my business, doing my thing. Some messages came to me while I was sleeping and whom did they come from? Our Angels!

I'm going to share with you some of my experiences of what happened with readings that I've done for the public over the years. What's really interesting is that some of the messages and advice that I give to clients while I'm doing a session with them, I am hearing for the very first time myself and when it's coming out of my mouth!!!

You will see and understand about a few angels and saints that I am personally drawn to, and that have made an impact in my life. To get their help, all you have to do is call out their name and ask for their help.

So, I wrote this book with passion with the intensions of soothing your heart and making your soul smile, letting you know that during your good moments of life but especially during your darkest times, there really are angels all around you and that God really does care about you. Just never give up, and have blind faith knowing you are always loved and never alone.

So, kick back, relax, and enjoy reading these interesting stories and poems.

Introduction

■ ■ ■

GOD WORKS IN MYSTERIOUS WAYS. Hmmmm… how it all began for me.

Going back when I was approximately 28 years old, I was very frustrated with my life. The strange thing was I had everything going in the right direction. I owned my own successful window cleaning/power washing business, I was married with a baby girl, nice house, nice cars, vacations, and yet, I was still feeling unfulfilled. One day I went downstairs to my home office and I'm looking up at my tiled ceiling and I said to God, "I need answers and I need CLEAR answers. Just don't scare the hell out of me when you pull through," LOL.

After that short conversation with God, I walked from my office to the kitchen and on my counter, was a bunch of junk mail just sitting there, rather than just throwing it all out I decided to look through it just to see if there was anything worth my while. Then I saw this postcard that read, "How would you like to develop your psychic ability and intuitiveness? Come to the Edgar Caycey Foundation in Virginia Beach for this one weekend seminar.

I thought to myself hmmmm, that's interesting I didn't know you could learn how to do this. I thought either you have it or you didn't. I asked my wife, who was my wife at that time, "Ya wanna go with me?" She said, "No, I have no interest in that stuff, you can go if you want but I'm not going." So, I signed up and I went!!

When I got there, there were about 50 people in the room from all over the U.S. Our teacher taught us how to open up our heart and mind to be 100% unconditional with any thoughts or images that may come to your mind and just share it with whatever partner you may be teamed up with. Don't hold back any information you may get regardless of how silly or stupid the images in your thoughts are. Just share it. It turned out I was pretty good at giving information to people I never met before, these people who I was reading could relate to a lot of what I was telling them. My God, I was so excited that I could do this that it blew me away. That this ability even existed!! ME; being able to tell people things about themselves without any knowledge of who they were. That was one awesome spiritual weekend.

When I went back home and I got myself a deck of spiritual cards at a spiritual shop and these cards are known as "Rune Cards." I started reading for my family and friends for free for a few years, just for the fun of it. People began telling me how accurate I was with my predictions. As well as reading cards, I was also taught by looking at someone's picture or holding an object of theirs (such as keys or a piece of jewelry) I'd be able to get images. Even if I have to say so myself I was pretty damn good at calling shots for these people.

There was a time in my life where I saw these two stocks and I really felt they were going to take off so I borrowed $20,000.00 from two friends and I told them within one year I would pay them back with 10% interest. So, one year goes by and I'm out $5,000.00!!! I'm freakin out! So now I need to pay back the $20,000.00 to my original investors and borrow $5,000.00 from another friend to cover the $5,000.00 loss. Plus, I needed to take $2,000.00 of my own money to cover the interest I promised to my friends who lent me the money. Now I'm really frustrated, WHY? Because the moment I sold both stocks, both of them started to take off, going higher and higher in price. One of them went up 100% and the other one went up 650%!!! All within 6 months' time! You have no clue how angry I was… so now after losing $7,000.00 and seeing my stocks go up, I'm sitting on my living room couch incredibly frustrated and I say out loud to myself, "What can I do to make up this kind of loss and make extra money?" I lay my head back and I thought, "Ya know what? I know how to do readings. I'll throw an ad in the paper and I'll have it say: 'If I don't pull thru for you, no charge.'" It turns out 90% of the people paid me, and a whole new world opened up for me. **That loss in the stock market was the biggest gain of my life!**

Now, 28 years later, I have counseled and read for over 20,000 people and God knows I'm a very driven person and the way to get me going is to put my back against the wall to get my wheels spinning on how to make more money. The funny thing is growing up I always wanted to be a counselor or a therapist, but I didn't have the brain power or patience to deal with books and the money wasn't available for me to go to college. What's really cool, NOW that I have developed my gift and have been blessed by God and the Angels, I now have therapists that come to see me for answers.

I was raised in a Kosher Jewish home, however as I got older my beliefs became more spiritual than religious. When my family first found out I was doing readings no one believed I could do it. They didn't believe I could make predictions about peoples' future. So, this one time after years of reading people, I'm sitting in my parents' living room watching TV as my father is reading the newspaper. He puts down the paper and he looks at me with a smile, and laughing he says, "Arthur, do you really read people or are you just bullshitting them." I laughed so hard because my own Dad had a hard time conceiving the fact that I can actually see the future and talk to angels and dead people.

My family only started to believe in me when they heard me on 101.5 one of New Jersey's top radio stations. They figured if I'm good enough to get on that station then I gotta have some kind of talent. How I got on that station, I was doing a psychic party at my friend Susan's home and this one lady Debbie comes downstairs into Susan's finished basement where I'm doing the readings for everyone individually, and she looks at me VERY SKEPTICALLY and she looks at me with a smile and says, "So what do you have to tell me?" I started with her son, I said, "Your son is going to start to complain about his one wrist hurting him." She said, "My son's wrist doesn't bother him at all." He never complained about it. Then I said, "He's going to have to go to the dentist and get major work done on one of his teeth, and they are not going to get it right on the first time, he's going to have to go back 1 or 2 times to have it fixed properly." She said, "My son has perfect teeth and my father is our dentist, you don't know what you are talking about, go ahead what else you got?" I said your son is going to change his major or minor to Philosophy. She said, "MY SON? Philosophy!!! YOU have never been more wrong in your whole life. What do you see for my daughter?" I said, the two of you fight like cats and dogs, but when she moves out the two of you will get along just fine. She said, "OK, I'll give you that one. What do you see with my job?" I see you will continue to do well and one of your bosses is going to leave or get fired. "Really!?!" she said, "What about my relationship?" My reply was in August either your relationship will move way up from where you are now or you're going to break up, but I think you'll break up with him. "We get along great; you don't know what you're talking about." So, Debbie ended up walking away saying this was the worst reading ever.

Well what ended up happening was her son began to complain about his wrist hurting from his job. He went to the dentist for a root canal and they didn't clean it all out correctly the first time, he had to go back 2 additional times. In the middle of the school year, her son brought home a whole new set of books and told her he switched his minor to philosophy. Two months later her boss was fired, she broke up with her boyfriend in August, and when her daughter moved out for college the relationship improved tenfold.

At the time Debbie happened to be the #1 salesperson at New Jersey 101.5 and told Craig Carton (who was the top radio personality at that time), "You have to get this guy Artie on your show, he's Amazing!" And that's how I got on this station.

How I got my first radio gig ever, I hired this woman Sierra who was originally selling advertising space to me with her spiritual magazine that she worked for and I ended up hiring her as my manager and she is the one who ultimately persuaded Joe Kelly the program director to get me on 107.3 FM CAT Country Radio. I was only supposed to be on that station for a one-time appearance. After I left the studio, which is out of the Atlantic City area, I received a call from Joe, and he said "Artie I have something to tell you." "Go ahead," I replied. "Well after you left our station, we received 22 people calling in wanting to speak with you. How would you like to be on our station every week for a few minutes? We can do it by phone on a three-way conversation." "Great" was my response. It's now over 9 years later and I'm still on

CAT Country Radio. I owe so much to Joe Kelly and CAT Country for launching my career, and I am thankful for the friendship we share.

I have also been on Philadelphia's hottest country station, 92.5 FM WXTU, along with FOX TV "The Q Show" Philadelphia channel 29.

With ALL the blessings of God and help from my Angels, I have been able to predict events before they happen. I have given people accurate medical advice and described to people of what's going on in their bodies. Even though I never got a college education I do tell people I went to the University of Boston and Maryland but that was just to visit my friends. Lol!! I have given thousands of people medical, legal, and love advice; and it was all from the help of my angels feeding me answers. (I am not a doctor, nor do I claim to be. Always refer to a doctor for medical advice.)

I have described people's future love lives with extreme accuracy, I have told people outcomes of events and relationships, and I have given out outcomes of winning financial gains. I have communicated to people's loved ones who have passed away. I have told people accurate information about their pets, living or deceased.

And I get all my answers from the Spiritual World.

THANK YOU GOD!!!

It Makes Me Laugh

■ ■ ■

It makes me laugh when people tell me they don't believe in God. I say to them:

"So, when your kid sneezes, instead of saying God Bless You, what do you say… better luck next time?"

Ego versus The Soul

■ ■ ■

Your ego will do in the moment for instant gratification.
Your soul will guide you upon what's best for you in the long run and the overall good.
Your ego sees only what's in front of you.
Your soul will allow you to have complete awareness to understand beyond immediate appearances.
Your ego will defend your actions.
Your soul will ask for forgiveness.
Your ego can keep you emotionally off-balance.
Your soul will give you harmony and balance.
Your ego lives in fear.
Your soul lives for love and to be happy.
God loves you unconditionally and blesses you with free will for you to make your own choices.
Amen.

Let the Truth Set You Free

■ ■ ■

LEARN TO LOVE YOURSELF. THAT is the key to happiness.

Your ego and your soul are always at battle with one another.

Your ego says that it's better and easier to meet up to other peoples' expectations rather than accommodate your own needs. Why rock the boat? Let's make everyone else happy instead.

Your soul is screaming:

"I'm not happy and if you don't start making me happy, your body is going to get totally stressed out; aches and pains and disease are going to occur. I'm telling you, there is going to be hell to pay if you don't start listening to me, YOUR SOUL and INNER SPIRIT."

Your ego is saying, "Just play the pretend game on the surface that everything is OK and lets just keep on making everyone else's needs and happiness more important than ours. This way we are going to be liked more and approved of by others. Oh, you can handle it, besides you can always just tell little white lies and tell people what they can handle, rather than being raw honest with them… less hassle, less fighting. Let's just accommodate everyone and forget about ourselves."

Your soul is screaming:

"Honor thyself! Love thyself! Respect thyself!"

Why does everyone get to be happier than me?!!

Let's live in our own truth and accommodate everyone under OUR terms.

I no longer want to chase after anyone else's approval. The people who love me unconditionally will stand by me, appreciate me, love me, and accept me for who I am. The people who want to judge me, get mad at me, or ridicule me because I'm not doing what they expected of me, I have no problem releasing them out of my life. Just love and respect me the same way that I love and respect you and myself, and we will always be in one another's lives.

I have decided that I am going to live in my own truth. I am no longer going to give more value of other people's thoughts and opinions over mine, unless they have my best interest at heart.

Whether I am right or wrong, my feelings are not debatable; my feelings are my truth and I must honor them to be happy. I am not ashamed to say I deserve the best out of life, I am #1, and I love myself. When I say that I love myself, I am not saying that I'm better than anyone else, and I am not saying it to sound or be cocky. I am honoring myself and I will love you as much as I love myself, as long as you respect me in the same way I respect you.

When I have pure love and respect for myself, I am a much happier person. When I am happier, I am a stronger person. When I am a stronger person, I can help others in a larger capacity while still satisfying my own needs. When you live in your own truth, you experience the meaning of the saying:

LET THE TRUTH SET YOU FREE.

When you live in your own truth, that's what gives your soul freedom and happiness.

NAMASTE

The Soul that Searched in the Mirror

■ ■ ■

You say you're strong,
But yet you can't express your true feelings.
You say you don't deserve happiness,
But yet you're always looking for it.
You say you have nothing in your life or nothing to live for,
But yet you're willing to fight tooth and nail for the nothing you have.
You say you want a change for yourself,
But yet you move ever so slowly.
You say you have faith in God,
But yet you don't trust the unknown to turn out for the best.

You express yourself with bitterness and anger, and get little results
And somehow you understand when feelings are expressed to you with
love and compassion.
Why can't you share love and compassion with others?
You say I don't know how much longer I can go on.
I say trust the Lord he'll let you know when it's time to rest.

You live for quantity,
And complain there is no quality.
Stop and smell the roses
Love is all around you.
You just never stopped to notice.

If you're trying to hold up a building that can't stand on its own
You're wasting your time and the land that it sits on.
Start fresh and build a new foundation for yourself and from there let the
new begin.

There's no need for you to lie to yourself
Just follow your heart's desire and you'll always be happy.

With love,
Your Guardian Angel

You Are a Beautiful Person, Honor Yourself

■ ■ ■

A LOT OF PEOPLE HAVE a tough time accepting love and compliments from other people and the majority of the time it's because they didn't or aren't receiving love and appreciation from the person they wanted it from the most. Whether from their parents, siblings, kids or significant other, their spirit becomes so beaten down by not receiving the acknowledgement and approval from the closest people to them. As a result, they find themselves always chasing after other people's approval.

So many times, they become major people-pleasers, trying to make everyone else happy, and trying to meet up to the expectations of others. They put everyone else's needs before their own, usually at their own expense. They have a hard time with time management, trying to please too many people in doing things in a very short period of time. They over-extend themselves and end up making empty promises they can't keep.

Another thing people of this nature do is they have a habit of giving away more money to their loved ones than what they can afford. People of this nature will take the money they need that's supposed to pay for their own bills, food or any other responsibilities they may have, and give those funds that they themselves need so desperately to someone else, in hopes of fixing the other person's problems and making their lives easier.

By doing so, not only are you disrespecting yourself, but you are now creating a dependency of these people you are trying to help, and their appreciation then turns into expectations. When the time comes and you can no longer keep up with others expectations, the happiness you created for them turns into anger or resentment. Thus, making you feel responsible or guilty because you feel you let them down. The reality of it: all those people you're trying to help put themselves in their own position through their own personal choices. Now you are allowing yourself to get caught up in the karma that they created for themselves.

To avoid all these negative feelings where you want to help other people, you have to honor yourself, and make yourself #1 while you are taking care of others. What do I mean by this?

With the money you have or make, take care of YOUR necessities first. Pay all your own bills, make sure you have enough food for yourself, and then if you have any money left over after that, if you want to help out others by all means go ahead and knock yourself out. When it comes to giving your time, stop trying to force two pounds of baloney in a one pound bag by over-extending yourself.

Take the stress out of your life by learning to say "NO." If you can't provide for their needs given the time frame you have within your comfort zone then learn to say, "No, I will, just not now, or I can do it later." If you can't accommodate others in their timing when they want it, one of two things will happen: either they will wait for you or they will try another person who may be able to meet their needs. And there you go! The pressure is off of you. If you have people who are relentless and continue to push you, you need to stand your ground. Don't allow their needs to take precedence over yours.

The only time these rules don't apply is when you're dealing with an emergency situation, you stop what you are doing to handle the matter, of whatever it takes to get matters handled properly. There is a difference between taking care of an emergency situation and overly accommodating others as a way of life.

"Spiritual Vampires" are people who constantly want to speak to you on the phone many times a day or for long periods of time. They will suck the life out of you if you let them. If your phone rings and you see it's someone that gets on your nerves, let them leave a message. If you don't have the quality time and/or the quality energy to give, let it go into voice-mail. Return the call when you can comfortably afford to share your time on your own terms.

The moral of this:

"Honor and Love Thy self!"

The Naked Soul, Understanding the Naked Truth

■ ■ ■

The naked soul,
That stands for truth and unconditional love.
The naked soul,
That leaves itself open, trusting that God's kindness and love will protect over it.
The naked soul,
Which stands for the highest level of truth to itself and God.

When the soul is masked by the human body, shouldn't the soul stay truthful to itself and God?
The body was meant as a form of communication from one soul to another while in human form. So many people have used the body as a mask to cover its true identity.

When one person is being judged by another, how sad is it that the person who is being judged is trying to live up to the expectation of others, rather than be true to him or herself? Shouldn't all souls just love one another for who they are? And not be wrapped up in fear and expectations? I'm not sure... will I ever be accepted for who I am and how I really feel?

I can't believe it!
I was buying into other people's expectations of me and their perception of me wasn't even accurate. I even forgot who I really am, because I got lost in their fears for a moment in time and I allowed their fears to become mine.

Take off this mask you call the human body so that my soul can be free.

Now I can feel the unconditional love of God, of how life was really meant to be. I no longer have to live my life according to anyone else's expectations but my own. I take responsibility for my choices. I just want to love and be loved while having fun doing it. Deep down my heart and soul are good and because of the unconditional love that God has for me, I'm free of guilt and shame.

If I am drop of water from God's ocean,
Doesn't that make me a part of the powerful force of what the ocean is?
If God is filled with compassion and unconditional love, and my soul is a part of him,
Then why should I fear God, the Holy Spirit of Unconditional Love, or anyone else? For God has no expectation of me, He just loves me.

I now understand that regardless of how I live my life, I'm truly loved and accepted for just who I am,
And why not?
I am a part of God, as God is a part of me;
We're partners in life.
I thank God and you for your unconditional love.

Only Allow Positive People into Your Life

■ ■ ■

IT IS NOT NECESSARY TO hang onto every single relationship in your life if they are no longer serving a positive purpose to you or if you don't feel comfortable in their company. Even though there are certain people who have been in your life for many, many years, if they are spiritually and emotionally sucking your energy dry, it is time for you to honor yourself and let them go out of your life, or at least as much as possible, if not all together.

It brings your energy level way down when you allow yourself on a daily basis to keep on bitching and complaining about other people or circumstances you don't like.

Friends and/or lovers will come and go out of your life and each person brings a valuable lesson, whether it is positive or negative, business or personal. It is up to you how many times you wish to repeat a physical or emotional experience to happen over and over again. A good part of the quality of our life is determined by the kind of people we choose to surround ourselves with, or the environment we allow ourselves to hang out in.

If you have really good news you wish to share with someone, do not share your good news with just anyone, especially those who usually have a negative comment or nothing nice to say about anyone or anything. Those friends or family members who have a tendency to bring you down or have a jealous nature, you don't want to share your good news with them because misery loves company. Only share your good news with those people who truly wish the best for you and are in your corner supporting you. Allow their enthusiasm to keep the momentum of your good news going.

When it comes to family, they are a part of your life whether you like it or not. There are family members that you look to keep in contact with on a daily or regular basis and there are those family members who you love but don't like. Those are the kind of people you might feel obligated to see only during special events or occasions. The right thing to do is just to be cordial and just keep the conversation light. If they are the type of people who don't make you feel good then it's perfectly normal and okay to keep in touch with them a few times a year, once a year, once every other year, or sometimes not at all.

If someone you love or care about does not want to heal or is not ready to heal from an emotional problem, then you need to let it go. It is not just about you, but it is about where they are at within their own head. You can't control how other people feel, but you can control how you choose to deal with the other person or situation. That's the only thing you have control over.

Sometimes writing a letter of compassion to the other person trying to bury the hatchet can possibly help heal the situation between the two of you. If they are not ready to compromise with you or to hear you out, again, you have to let it go. You can't force it; you can't force someone to do something they do not want to do, no matter how hard you try.

Sometimes we are stuck in a situation where we are forced to care for someone within our family who is not physically or emotionally able to take care of themselves. The burden is left on your shoulders. The best thing for you to do is to try to delegate some responsibility to other family members or ask some friends if they can help out, or hire someone to give you a break from your responsibilities. If you find yourself in a constant, negative environment that you almost can't get out of, then play upbeat or some kind of pleasant music that you appreciate. Maybe go to the park, to the beach… wherever you find serenity. Watch a good comedy, go out in nature, or maybe have a nice walk around the mall. Sometimes you just want time for yourself, and to be someplace quiet. Take a long drive just for the hell of it, take a bubble bath or relax in a room with candlelight. Pick up a hobby, play music or do something else that might be creative that you would find to be fun. Reach out to people who you really appreciate, who maybe you haven't heard from in a long time.

Positive thoughts plus positive actions equal positive results. Negative thoughts plus negative actions equal negative results. It's your free will, and it's your choice on how you wish to create the quality of your life based on what's given to you. You can put energy into complaining about your problems or you can put energy into creating the solutions of your problems. The truth of the matter is that it's all up to you.

Beware: people who share gossip and rumors with you about other people are the same people who will gossip about you to others, so be careful of what news you choose to share with those kinds of people because it will come around and bite you in the ass.

I was raised if you don't have something nice to say about others then don't say anything at all.

Just When You Thought No One Cared

■ ■ ■

NOT ENOUGH PEOPLE IN THIS world respect and appreciate God and life, as they should. Too many people bring their own lives down into ruins along with others, and it's not until they've lost everything that they turn to God with a cry of help, and God says to them:

"I was with you all along, you didn't have to wait until you hit rock bottom to know that I care about you.

Harmony and happiness are always within your reach; you just have to move in that direction. As long as you have the resources, but you continued on your journey to pain, even though it was away from where you belong. I let you keep on going because I love you unconditionally and I gave every soul 'free will' to move in the direction of their choices. Whatever you desire, you shall receive. I give you the opportunity to express life whichever way you choose to live it… in pain or in happiness. When you've experienced enough pain and all of your resources have totally diminished, I'll be waiting for your call.

I love you just as much where you are right now in life as you were when you first began. When you feel the pain of life from the choice you've made, I feel your pain with you. When you feel the joy of life from the choice you've made, I feel your happiness along with you. You are never alone or not loved, regardless of your choices in life. When you experience life, you experience me: The Lord Your God.

How you choose to experience your life is all up to you. Let go of living in fear and allow the flow of love to enter your heart and I promise you a lifetime of happiness."

Love Always,
God

Acceptance Brings Healing

■ ■ ■

Too MANY TIMES PEOPLE ALLOW others or situations to get the best of them, which they have no control over. How many times have you remained angry, hurt or disappointed over someone that no matter what you say to them or no matter what you do for them, they continue to act in a very stubborn or selfish manner?

If you say up, they say down.

If you say the sky is blue, they say the sky is green.

If you say something positive about what you are doing or something nice about a situation or someone else, they have a negative twist on everrreeething!!!

They always wanted to debate you. They say they are going to be there for you at a particular time, and they're always running late or not showing up. They say they're going to help you and they don't.

Misery breathes negativity, and misery loves company.

So, here's my advice to you:

Before you allow yourself to be in the company of a person who is a downer, don't allow yourself to be on their emotional negative stage. Don't allow yourself to become a part of their Negative Energy! It's not about you; it's about them! That's who they are by nature. Only observe them being who they are. Look at them with compassion like a bird with a broken wing. No matter how much you disagree with them, don't feed into their conversation. You'll only get more upset when you're trying to prove yourself right and them wrong. Would you rather be right? Or would you rather be happy?

Anytime you have positive or happy news you want to share, NEVERRRR tell your good news to people who are negative or "Gossip Queens." Only share your good news with people who are "Pro You," people who are genuinely happy for you. It doesn't matter if they are family or what you consider to be close friends, if you know that certain people around you are jealous-natured or negative, KEEP your mouth shut around them. They will burst your bubble or make you depressed. If you're smart, you'll start to disconnect yourself from these people who don't appreciate you.

It's not necessary for you to hang onto every relationship in your life if they don't serve a positive purpose or energy. If you feel stuck with certain people, you can't change them but you can change whom you choose to be with or how you allow them to affect you.

If you want to hang with people who are like friendly puppy dogs, then hang out with those people who make you feel loved or appreciated. Are you hanging out with people who are like snakes or alligators and expecting them to be warm, loving, or fuzzy? FAHGETABOWDIT!!! It's not happening, they're reptiles! Reptiles aren't warm, cuddly and nurturing. It's not about you; it's who they are by nature!

When you look at people who tend to be like this by nature, try to notice why they are like that, given their backgrounds. Some people don't know how to love because of their bad experiences growing up with their families. Maybe they were abused, or their parents were bad role models, maybe they were hurt in past relationships. Certain people can only love in the best way they know how, if at all. They may not love the same way you do or in the way that you may like.

It's up to you to answer, "Do I still want this person in my life?" Do the pros outweigh the negative or vise a versa?

The key awareness is "ACCEPTANCE."

So, either accept people for who they are and adjust yourself accordingly, or start cleaning up the quality of your life in relationships and block out the negative people who you've allowed to be a part of you for so long.

God gave us "Free Will" … it's your choice! Who, what, and how you choose is up to you; it's your life.

Why God, Why?

■ ■ ■

I CAN'T HELP BUT NOTICE everyone I've met who says they don't believe in God are usually the ones who experience a lot of heartache in their lives, whether it be emotional or physical setbacks. These people who say they don't believe in God usually carry anger or resentments within their heart. The exception to this rule: people who happen to be Atheist or Agnostic where they don't carry that kind of anger are scientists and philosophers because their mindset is more from a theory point of view.

Some people might ask: is there really an almighty, compassionate, loving God then why doesn't he stop mean people from doing harm? Why doesn't he stop wars from happening? Why did he take my loved one away from me so soon, so early in my life? Why does he not do something to stop the pains of the world? Why does he allow people and animals to suffer?

You should understand everything has a flip side. Where there is joy, there are heartaches and vise a versa. The reason why God doesn't stop things from happening is because he created "free will" and with Free Will, he allows everything to happen – joy as well as evil. By our own Free Will, we get to choose what we want to experience in life.

So, you may think that God doesn't care about you, or all of humanity and Mother Nature, but there is a big reason why things happen in the way they do that is beyond what our human brain can understand or comprehend. You might think that God doesn't care about you or your vulnerable circumstance in life, but that's not true. Do you think that

God didn't care when Jesus was being beaten and hung on the cross? God doesn't stop anything from happening; because of Free Will, he allows all possibilities to happen.

God allowed the Jewish people to suffer for hundreds of years in slavery and then allowed Moses and the Jews to stay and wander in the desert for 40 years before entering the land of Israel. You don't think God loves Jewish people or black people who suffered in slavery?

John Lennon of the Beatles wrote songs on love and having a peaceful world. He sang songs about unconditional love, and John was shot coldheartedly for no reason. You don't think God loved and appreciated John Lennon? When Martin Luther King and Malcom X wanted peace through peaceful demonstrations, both were shot to death. Mandela was wrongfully put in jail for many years for demonstrating peace. God never stopped any of these crazy acts of violence and cruelty.

You don't think God loves these people who were filled with love and peace in their heart? In the Bible when Lucifer took everything away from Jobe, his family and his flock, Jobe was God's most loyal follower. God didn't stop this horrific act from happening and God rewarded Jobe for remaining dedicated to him with another beautiful family, more land, and more of a herd. God created Free Will for everything and anything to happen, the bad as well as the good. Through our prayers, we keep our faith and share our love with others. God will not only see us through our pain, but he will fulfill our hearts and bless us with abundance.

Just because pain and evil exist, that doesn't mean that God, Love, and His Glory don't exist.

God rewards everyone in some way when people show and express their love and commitment of blind faith. The understanding of having blind faith is when you can still continue to be a good and loving person, even when the face of pain and/or evil might show up in your life.

It makes me laugh inside when I hear people say how much they believe in God and that they pray every day and go to church every week. In the next breath, they tell me how nervous they always are about their life or their family and friends.

My response to them is "You might believe there is a God, but you don't believe in God." Some of these people who I say this to, these people who pray all the time or go to church every week or have religious artifacts around their neck, become offended by this comment. How can you tell me you believe in God when you are constantly walking around in fear and worry? It makes no sense! Fear is the opposite of love and love is God. If you really believe in God, then you should know God has everything under control. You are sitting or walking around worrying all the time in negative thought, saying I'm afraid of this and I'm afraid of that is not going to solve anything. THIS, I call negative prayers. You send out negative energy to those you care about when you say you are always worried or nervous for them. Start saying or praying,

"Thank you God for sending all your beautiful blessings to me, my friends and family. Thank you for always watching over us and protecting us from all kinds of harm. Thank you for bringing the best outcome possible for our higher wellbeing. In the Name of the Holy Spirit, Amen."

A Promise Is a Promise, or Is It

■ ■ ■

IT'S NOT REALISTIC FOR SOMEONE to say, "I promise you" when talking about a future circumstance. Reason being, you never know when situations may change out of your control that may either delay you or keep you from fulfilling your promise/word of honor "I promise you."

Your intention in that given moment is yes, I will pull through for you, and I will be there for you. The reality is if I can, if time allows me, if I don't get held off by anyone or anything, if my finances allow, if my feelings don't change, if my job allows, if the traffic doesn't delay me, if my conscience doesn't guilt the hell out of me, if people pull through for me, then yes, I will pull through for you, on my promise, "I promise."

A true statement to say to anyone based on a promise is "I promise I will do my best to pull through." Now the person who is receiving of your words, "I promise you," are taking your words as a 100% guarantee. The receiver's mindset on your promise is "come hell or high water, you are going to pull through for me at all costs." When the receiver of a promise invests their emotions 100% on your word, they are setting themselves up for a possible huge disappointment; "I am putting all my trust in you that you will pull through on your promise." If someone has no intention of pulling through on their word then that person has no right to say, "I promise you," under those circumstances.

Just because you or anyone else wants to pull through on their word, doesn't mean a 100% guarantee that you're going to pull through. It's just your intentions to pull through in that given moment. The only time a person is capable of being 100% true to their words of a promise is when something has already happened or they are in the process of doing it in that moment. For example, I promise you, I am telling the truth... I promise you, I didn't do it... I promise you, I delivered the package. I promise you, I'm cleaning my room as we speak. When it comes to relationships, being honest and pulling through on your words and having open communication is just as important as love.

Even though you may love somebody at a perfect 10, if you do not have trust, you do not have a relationship or at least a healthy one. Be careful what you promise to other people. Trust is like a tree: it takes time to grow and only one moment to cut it down. Trust and respect cannot be forced, it's earned.

A Promise Is a Promise,
Or Is It!

The only time a promise is a guaranteed promise is when you are explaining a factual truth to someone based on what has already happened or is happening in the given moment.

The Pain and Beauty of Religion

■ ■ ■

Deepak Chopra once said:

"Religion is other peoples' experiences
Spirituality is one's own experiences."

How FUNNY/IRONIC IT IS THAT the number one reason why wars breakout is over religion. No one religion is better than the other. No one religion is the only way to get to heaven. Whatever feels right to you in your heart and soul about how you wish to perceive, relate, and express yourself to God and/or the Universe, then that's the perfect religion for you.

Even if your family and peers think and feel differently than you do. If you have your own special way or your own ritual on how you wish to pray to God and if it feels right to you then "don't change!" As long as you have love and respect in your heart towards God and your fellow man, that's all that matters.

Being that I was born and raised in a Jewish upbringing, there have been Christians and Born Again Christians who have said to me that I am lucky because according to some Bibles we, the Jewish people, are the "Chosen Ones." And in the next breath, they tell me if I don't believe and follow Jesus I won't go to heaven.

How is that statement possible?

Jesus, Moses, Abraham, Mary and Joseph were all Jews and they're not going to heaven? Oh my God!

Believing in Jesus as your Savior is one way to respect life and God, but not the only way...

Again, having love and respect within your heart towards God, yourself, and your fellow man is probably the most spiritual and religious way to be.

Why should you never stop believing in God? Because he never stops believing in you!

The Hypocrites of Religion

■ ■ ■

THERE WAS A BLACK FAMILY that moved to Georgia in the early 1960's and one Sunday morning this handsome black gentleman went to look for a church that he and his family could belong to. He goes to the first church and there was a sign on the door, "No colored people allowed." He went to the second church in town and the sign said, "We do not welcome black people." He tried one more time to go to another church nearby and a tall fellow stood at the door. As the man approached to enter the church, the man at the door stuck his arm out and said, "Sorry sir, we don't allow black people in our church."

The black man felt so rejected he sat at the bottom of the walkway of the church by the street with his face in his hands and with tears in his eyes. After a few minutes, he heard God's voice speak to him and God said, "Leroy, what's the matter my son?" Leroy replied, "God, I'm trying to express my love and prayers to you and they won't let me in." God responded, "Don't feel bad my son, they don't even let me in."

God's love is unconditional and God does not judge nor is he a prejudice spirit.

My parents raised my two brothers and me to be kind, loving, and respectful to others and to God. I 100% believe in my heart and soul anyone who incorporates within this way of living and thinking will end up in heaven, regardless of what religion you choose. God does not need our prayers; we need God to hear our prayers. Through our gratitude and prayers, God will bless us with his love, miracles and blessings that will benefit our lives, as well as our family and friends. Amen.

We Are All the Children of God

■ ■ ■

ONE OF MY JEWISH FRIENDS once asked me, "Is Jesus really the son of God?" He said he was having a hard time buying that concept. "What do you think about that idea, Artie?" In the moment I didn't have a clear answer, "Let me meditate on that for a moment," I said.

As I sat back quietly, my angel explained:

Jesus is the Son of God, but no more than you and I. You're the Son of God, I'm the Son of God, and we are all the sons and daughters of God. Jesus just happens to be more highly evolved in the understanding of what love and life itself is all about. He came upon this earth to share with all of us wisdom, and unconditional love through his words and his actions. He was one of the many teachers to teach us the importance of blind faith, compassion for others, being forgiving, and the healing abilities of what unconditional love can do when being expressed. The importance of caring, kindness, and loving one another is what his and other highly evolved souls were all about. What a beautiful gift God has given all of us to have such highly evolved souls come to us with such love and wisdom, as well as the gift of sending us angels to help us get through our challenges in life.

We Are All One

■ ■ ■

WHENEVER I HEAR THE EXPRESSION "We are all one," this is my perception and understanding of its meaning: when you look at the ocean, it's a very powerful and beautiful force of nature. Each one of us represents a drop of water within the ocean. Each drop carries the DNA of the entire ocean. Every drop of water put together is as one and IS the ocean. The ocean is God and we are all connected to each other within the God force.

When you allow yourself to be as one and to be a part of the big beautiful energy of the life force, you have all the love and power of nature working on your behalf. For people who choose to separate themselves from believing in God and choose to keep themselves separate from others, they usually feel depressed, angry, bitter, and alone because they choose not to be a part of the powerful loving force of God and society.

If you took an empty cup and scooped out some water from the ocean, the water in the cup has become powerless by being on its own. Throw the cup of water back in the ocean, and that water has now become powerful again. Now you have included yourself back in the powerful force of nature and society. You consciously now have all the love and power working in your favor, because you made yourself a part of the positive force, the positive energy of God's love and his world.

What I Wish Lord

■ ■ ■

Dear Lord,
Give me the strength and endurance of a weed,
Where I can grow vibrant and strong under any and all circumstances,
Regardless of my surroundings!

May I end up blossoming like a bouquet of flowers,
As I mature and grow through the journey of life.

I wish to touch as many lives as possible,
Where I can make a positive impact on people,
And bring smiles and happiness upon their lives.

When someone walks away from me
I wish for them to say,
God, I'm really glad I met that person.

Dear Lord,
Thank you for sharing your love with me,
Now I can share your love with others.
Amen.

The Perception of Life

■ ■ ■

EVERYTHING IN LIFE IS NOTHING more than our perception; all of life's situations are as big as it is or as small as it is, according to how you look at it. If you have a tendency of making every little thing a big deal, then more than likely you're probably living a very stressful life. If you downplay matters not to be a big deal or you learn to accept matters for what they are and deal with it calmly and maturely, the stress level within your body and life are going to be way down. Regardless of how you look at the particular situation, it still is what it is. It's just the energy you give it that makes something horrible or not so bad or pretty good.

Example: Neil Donald Walsh once said, "If you are in your home and you look up at the ceiling while downstairs, and then you walk upstairs to that same location, that piece of wood you are standing on is now a floor. The piece of wood never changed, it still is what it is, only your perception of the wood changed. From downstairs, that piece of wood is the ceiling and from upstairs that same piece of wood is the floor."

A beautiful girl in Jamaica came up to me and she said, "You want to know something Mun? In Jamaica we have no big problems, we only have small situations."

If you look at every problem in life like it's resolvable then it's really not a problem, it's a challenge that's resolvable. If you look at a situation with fear that there is no way out, then you have a problem on your hands. Because with that perception, you have just sentenced yourself to imprisonment for life. You have two options: either you give yourself parole by working on matters that can improve your situation to make life better, or you can get yourself out of your situation all together and start new beginnings.

Making changes in your life for the better and going through transformation can be very scary and painful, but your alternative is to keep things the same and have a life sentence of misery. That choice is yours; don't blame anyone or anything else while you're stuck. It is your choice to either listen to your gut or listen to what other people choose for you. The reality is you're never really stuck, it's only your perception that you are. It might take time and a certain amount of money to get you to where you want to be, but so long as you work on a plan to improve your matters on a daily basis, you will eventually be in a place of happiness where you belong. It comes down to how bad do you want happiness for yourself, knowing you're going to have to deal with the inconveniences of transformation that will get you to the place you want to be.

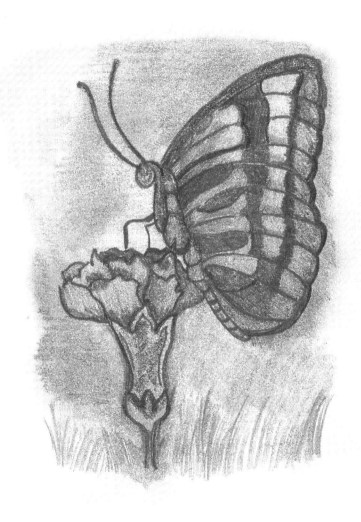

We Are Responsible for Our Choices

■ ■ ■

WHAT'S THE PURPOSE OF FREE will when there are certain things in our life that are Pre-Destined?

Before we were physically born into this world, we choose the challenges of our life. We choose our parents, as well as how and when we are going to leave this world. We already know the major players with whom we will encounter in our lives, such as family, friends, lovers, acquaintances, along with business associates. Everyone brings a lesson to our lives as we bring lessons to others. Our Spirit guides and angels assist us with the choices we make; however, the ultimate decision of what we choose to experience is our own. As soon as we are born into this world, we are blessed with amnesia. So now it's time to play the game of life according to all the pieces we have picked.

Why would we pick out such incredible challenges in our lives? The reason being we choose such hard experiences is to teach us about being unconditional with our love, to be forgiving, to have blind faith, and to learn about compassion. We go through these challenges so we can spiritually grow. In the spiritual world, our ultimate goal is to get to the highest level of heaven, and to get there is a part of the journey to experience such emotional and physical hardships, so we can understand to be unconditional with our love.

It's like trying to be a good boxer. If you want to be a really good boxer, you have to learn how to take a hard hit. The purpose of all the hard hits in life is to help us to become stronger and wiser. When you go through such hardships it's not God punishing you, but through all of your choices in life, the result is cause and effect. Meaning, whatever action you take will create a reaction, call it good, bad or indifferent. God loves all of us unconditionally, regardless of our choices, because our choices are nothing more than experiences.

The experience of Déjà Vu is when we have a recall of what we chose to experience while we were hanging out in the spiritual world before we were born into this lifetime, it then comes to our conscious mind as if it had already happened. An understanding of what had already been planned; a recall, a flashback of a concept of understanding of what was meant to be.

The bottom line is certain things are pre-destined to happen in our life while other situations are created by our own Free Will.

*Pre-Destiny is a course of events or certain people you are going to meet, no matter what. This is all a part of your experiences and challenges that you have personally chosen while you were in the Spiritual world prior to your birth.

**Free will is how you choose to allow all of these experiences to affect you, which gives you the quality of life, whether good, bad or indifferent. When God gave us the gift of Free Will, he does not stop you from making any decisions based upon your personal choices, whether it's loving or painful to you or others. If you choose to remain bitter and angry by your choice upon what you're dealing with, what's going to happen is you repeat your lesson until you come to terms with it and come to a place of acceptance and unconditional love.

Mind, Body & Spirit

■ ■ ■

SOMEONE ONCE ASKED ME, "Is the mind, body, and soul as one or are they separate?"

I sat there for a moment to ponder upon this question, in that moment I had no clue what the true answer was.

A minute later a voice came to me in my mind and it was explained to me like this:

Our mind creates, our body reacts, and our soul experiences and observes, however they all act as one unit.

Like a car, you have the wheels, the body of the car, steering wheel, transmission, and the engine; they are all separate, but act as one.

"Whether people might think you're right or wrong, your feelings are not debatable. Your feelings are always your truth. Thought is more from your brain than from your ego. Your feelings are an expression of your soul."

Regardless God Is Always There

■ ■ ■

GOD IS LIKE THE SUNSHINE on a cloudy day. Just because the clouds cover up the sunshine and you can't see it, that doesn't mean the sun isn't there. The sun is always shining. Sometimes when you can't see or feel the sun, that's just the clouds that act as fear creating doubt in our minds. God and the angels really are there for you, especially in your time of need. For people who doubt God in his existence, they think seeing is believing, not realizing when you start to believe then you'll start to see. Our minds work like a parachute, it only works when it's open.

Dear Lord,

 As I grow older I pray that I may have the love, patience, and wisdom of a saint and the playfulness and energy of a child.

Amen

A Few Remarkable Stories

■ ■ ■

Mooo

THIS LADY WANTS ME TO communicate to her deceased mother who she desperately misses. I was doing one of my Artie Parties (psychic party) at this one home. After her reading was over, she said to me, "Artie, some of the things you said to me were kind of general and a few things you said were specific, but I'm having a hard time believing that you were actually getting information from my mother."

"Alright, give me your mom's picture again and I'll see if she can give me a quick something for you." (I like to look at pictures of the deceased to communicate with them. When I look at the eyes of the deceased within the picture, the spirit communicates to me in my thoughts.) So, I'm looking at her mom's picture and I say to her, "Your mom is showing me a bunch of cows." "What do you want me to do with that?" she replied. In my eyes mind, I saw all the cows stand up and they were all mooing. "I don't know why I'm doing this," I started to Mooooooo out loud. This woman began to cry. "What's the matter?" I said. She pointed to her mom's picture and said, "That's her name." "What do you mean?" I was bewildered. "Her name is Muriel, but everyone calls her MOOO." I have to tell ya, I didn't see that one coming.

YOU SAVED MY LIFE

I came into the beauty salon and the girl who cuts my hair gave me a big hug and said, "Artie, you saved my life." I laughed because I thought she was either joking or exaggerating about a situation of some sort. Perplexed but smiling and laughing, I asked, "What happened that you say I saved your life?" She replied, "Last time you were here sitting in my chair, as I was cutting your hair, you looked at my reflection in the mirror and said I needed to go see a doctor right away, because you could see darkness over my shirt and in my chest area. I told you NO, you're probably seeing me with my mom; I take her once a month to see the doctor because of her health. You said Na, you felt it was me. I thought nothing of it.

The next time I took my mom to the doctors I asked him if he could quick check out my heart and he heard an irregular beat. They did an x-ray on me and found I had a blockage in one of my arteries; it was building to an aneurism. The doctor said that I was a walking time bomb and that if I didn't get checked out in that moment, I could have dropped dead at any moment. He gave me some kind of medication to thin my blood and clear my artery."

With that, she gave me another big hug and said, "Thank you so much Artie, you literally saved my life."

My Teeth

I was at the airport returning from Vegas, and I was literally just off the plane and walking through the corridor between the plane and the airport when a lady grabs my arm from behind and says, "Artie! Hi, I'm Sharon, you did a reading for me a few months ago and I have to thank you. You saved my teeth." I chuckled and smiled as I said, "How did I do that?" She replied, "You told me I needed to go to the dentist and that I have something going on in the upper part of my mouth on the right side," and she said, "I laughed because I have perfect teeth with no cavities! But I did make an appointment; he took x-rays of my mouth and he said that I had a bad infection within my gum, underneath my one tooth. He said that if I waited one more week, not only would I have lost that tooth, I would have lost both teeth on both sides of that one tooth because the infection was spreading that bad that fast! So, thank you Artie, thank you!" I got a big hug and a kiss on the cheek.

Birthday Numbers

I was doing an event for 40 women at this one café in Princeton, New Jersey. A couple of weeks later, the owner of the café called me and told me that I read for her best friend during that event. She said, "You told her that her mom is with her right now and that she is very proud of her for what she does for other people. You said that her mother told you, 'You need to play my birthday numbers in the lottery because they are coming out real soon.'" She continued to state that her friend did indeed play her mother's birthday numbers the next day. She WON! $6,200.00!! And that was her mother's gift to her. She does volunteer work and travels to other countries to do missionary work. "Wow Artie, what a great gift you have," said the café owner.

It's Me Mom!

■ ■ ■

THE STORY YOU'RE ABOUT TO read is truly one of the most spiritual experiences of my life. For about two weeks, I was constantly hearing about Lake George, NY. People all around me were talking about their Lake George vacations, which was out of the ordinary. It's a beautiful place, but you normally don't hear about it that often! Then I heard a radio-ad about it as well, so I finally decided to look into it. I called up my friend Dawn, who I haven't seen in a while, and asked her if she wanted to take the ride with me to Lake George. I told her that there was going to be a balloon festival happening on September 25th. At first, she said no, since she was already planning on riding in a bike a thon that Sunday. I informed her that I had to be back for Sunday too, since I had a psychic party booked for that day. We live in the Central Jersey area, so we agreed to leave early Saturday morning and come back late Saturday night.

As we were driving up the N.Y. Thruway Saturday morning around 6 am, Dawn looked out her window and said, "Oh Art, look at those beams of sunlight piercing through the clouds! It's so beautiful; I want to take a picture." So, I pulled over and told her, "You're going to see angels in that picture." I also couldn't help but notice that the three cars that just passed us on the highway all had the same numbers on their license plate. I keep an Angel Book in my car that tells me what numbers mean. I immediately looked up those numbers and it said, "You have extra angels surrounding you today." Sure enough, when we looked at the picture on her camera, there was Archangel Michael, charging at a Serpent with a baby in its own mouth. There was also another baby on the side watching, as well as other angels behind Michael for support. We were shocked and amazed at what we had just seen.

Shortly after seeing this beautiful site, we continued up the thruway and Dawn turned to me and said, "You know Art, today is the anniversary of my daughter's death." I told her, "I'm sure that she and the angels are letting you know that she's okay, and that she's around you."

We got to an airport in the Lake George area, where the hot-air balloons were supposed to lift off from. Unfortunately, it was too windy for the balloons to fly. Someone told us to come back at dusk, which was when they were going to try again. Not many people were around, except a few under the vendor tents where they were selling some cool trinkets. So being that we were only out there for the day, and waiting to see the balloons take off, we decided to drive a few miles to get to Lake George itself. Just as we were about to drive down a road off of Route 1 to get to the lake, I happened to look over to my left. There I saw "O.T.B." or Off Track Betting, a place where you can bet on horse racing without being at the tracks. So, I said to Dawn, "Do you wanna go inside the OTB and see if there's a horse with a name that represents your daughter? We will make a wager on it." She said, "Okay, sure!"

So, we went inside and were looking at six different programs, with all of the races that were going off at six different racetracks. As I was skimming down one of the programs, Dawn walks over to me with the program in her hand and says, "Hey Art, do you think this might be the horse we should bet on?" She pointed innocently to the horses' name on the program: "It's Me Mom."

I yelled out at the top of my lungs, "Are you kidding me?! Of course, this is the horse we are betting on! It's a sure thing! OH MY GOD!!"

We began to look at other horse names, and we saw one called "Hot Air." Dawn said, "I think we should bet on this one too because we're here to watch the balloons go up." I replied, "Good idea." Then we saw a horse called "Angel in Heaven." I was thinking, "Shit! I'm running out of money with all these bets."

We approached the betting booth and I enthusiastically told the fella behind the counter, "Bet on It's Me Mom; it's going to win." So, the fella said, "The race you want doesn't go off until 8 pm tonight, and our store closes at 4 pm." I replied, "You gotta be kidding me!" Then he said, "You know what? There's an OTB the next town over that closes at 10 pm. Go over there and you should be good." Dawn and I were extremely excited, and we hung out for the afternoon at the lake. They have restaurants, live music, and vendors; we were enjoying ourselves while waiting to go back to the local airport grounds to see the hot air balloons take off at dusk.

It became late in the afternoon, so we headed over to the balloon area of the airport grounds. As we got closer, there were cars parked everywhere… you would think that Bruce Springsteen was in town performing, that's how many cars there were. We had to walk about half of a mile to get to the grounds. Dawn and I managed to find a spot on the grass, and we laid down one blanket. Just as we were chilling like everyone else, waiting to see the balloons, Dawn happened to notice that there was a family sitting about fifty feet to our right. The parents were singing songs with their kids, and both kids had Down Syndrome. They were playing and singing and having a great time, and Dawn said, "My Britney, my daughter, she had Down Syndrome." To us, that was another sign that she was with us. It was the only family that had Down Syndrome kids amongst the thousands of people that were there, and we happened to be in the company of this wonderful, happy family.

About another hour went by before they announced that the balloons were not going to go off, since it was too cool and breezy. Even though the balloons were not going up, Dawn and I enjoyed hanging out. There were three sets of people who had balloons set up right near us, all within fifty yards of where we were sitting. Even though they did not launch their balloons to sail in the air, they were nice enough to fully inflate their balloons, so that the audience could see the beautiful balloons in all their glory. One balloon was more gorgeous than the next. They were HUGE!!

It was then time for Dawn and I to hit OTB before we headed home. As we were driving, Dawn and I were pretending to be in the mob, talking with New York accents to the tellers behind the window at OTB.

Me: "Excuse me sir, even though the race hasn't gone off yet, we need for you to pay us our winnings, IN advance. We know that our horse, 'It's Me Mom,' is going to win and we have a long drive home back to Jersey."

Dawn: "So I'm gonna ask you a question. Do you wanna live or do you wanna die? Now just give use our fricken money, so we can go home to our families. So, are you going to give us the money now? OR do we have to kill you?"

We were laughing our asses off at each other, while joking around with our Brooklyn accents. We were cracking a bunch of jokes and saying funny things to one another, the whole ride to OTB.

Once we arrived, we had about twenty minutes before our race would go off. Since we bet on three different horses in three different races, two of the races already ran, and we were just waiting for "It's Me Mom" to run in the seventh race. We went to the teller window to give him our two tickets to see how well our horses did. Our first horse "Angel in Heaven" lost, and the other horse "Hot Air" was scratched from the race. Since the horse never ran, they gave me back the $20.00 I had bet earlier. Dawn hit me on the shoulder and screamed, "Holy shit! That's another sign! The balloons never got off the ground today, and 'Hot Air' was scratched from the race!" So, we were both going crazy. We knew that "It's Me Mom" was going to win the upcoming race. I was yelling and screaming, and cracking jokes before the race went off. Dawn was biting her nails and pacing back and forth. She said, "I gotta step outside and have a cigarette. I'm way too nervous." I replied, "Damn! I'm telling you our horse is going to cross the finish line all by itself. No other horse is going to be close to our horse when it crosses the finish line!" So, after a few minutes went by, Dawn walked back into the building with a minute to go until race time. The both of us were staring at the TV. All of the horses were lining up at the gate with "It's Me Mom" as the number 10 horse.

ANDDDDD they're off!

Number 10 belted out of the gate first, and ran right in front of all the other horses; it was a short race that only went around ¾ of the track to the finish line. "It's Me Mom" took a commanding lead by three lengths, right from the get-go. "It's Me Mom" continued to pull away further and further ahead, and is now leading by six more lengths, the other horses looked like dogs compared to our horse! Unbelievable! "It's Me Mom" is now coming around into the home stretch has just taken a commanding 10 length lead and ended up crossing the finish line by an amazing 16 lengths!! Needless to say, Dawn and I were jumping around like crazy, yelling and screaming and going nuts! Our energy was through the roof! Between the both of us, we won a couple hundred dollars. I must tell you, it made our long ride home go much quicker and a lot more fun. Yahooo!!!

Britney was definitely with us that day and she showed it in so many ways! You gotta believe!!!

Picture 1:   Face and Body of Archangel Michael

Picture 2:   Sword

Picture 3:   Serpent with mouth open

Picture 4:   Baby Angel in Serpents mouth

Picture 5:   On Looking Young Child Looking at Archangel Michael

Picture 6 & 7: Angels of Support

Can Psychics or Mediums Read for Themselves?

■ ■ ■

FOR THE MOST PART, INTUITIVE people cannot read for themselves because when you are emotionally connected to the outcome of situations, as a spiritual being living the human experience, we don't know if the messages are coming through to us on a spiritual level or from our own ego. It's like a doctor trying to diagnose themselves. They are unable to, and they go to other doctors to get their needs taken care of. Same thing for psychics, we need outside counseling from someone who is not emotionally connected to our personal life, so we can hear the raw truth and get an outside perspective. It's more than healthy to get more than one person's point of view on what's going on in your life or any particular subject matter. Even therapists see other therapists to help balance out their own emotions.

The difference between a psychic/intuitive person and the general public is that a psychic knows to follow their first gut feelings and instincts. When thoughts or messages first come to them, they express or react according to that of which comes to them without overanalyzing the situation. Whereas when it comes to the general public, most people ignore their first gut feelings and choose to overanalyze what messages or thoughts first come to them.

Mother Teresa

■ ■ ■

"Teacher of unconditional love"

MOTHER TERESA TEACHES US TO help and love all human mankind regardless of race or creed. We are all one!

She dedicated her life to the poor and destitute.

"Do It Anyway"

"People are often unreasonable, irrational, and self-centered. Forgive them anyway.

If you are kind, people may accuse you of selfish, ulterior motives. Be kind anyway.

If you are successful, you will win some unfaithful friends and some genuine enemies. Succeed anyway.

If you are honest and sincere, people may deceive you. Be honest and sincere anyway.

What you spend years creating, others could destroy overnight. Create anyway.

If you find serenity and happiness, some may be jealous. Be happy anyway.

The good you do today will often be forgotten. Do good anyway.

Give the best you have, and it will never be enough. Give your best anyway.

In the final analysis, it is between you and God. It was never between you and them anyway."

The above prayer was on her wall at the Mother Teresa's Home for Children, located in Calcutta, India.

Mother Teresa teaches us to help and love all human mankind regardless of race or creed. We are all one!

She dedicated her life to the poor and destitute.

Padre Pio

■ ■ ■

"Saint of Miracles"

"STIGMATA" ARE THE CRUCIFIXION WOUNDS of Christ and beginning on September 20, 1918, Padre Pio had markings and was bleeding from his hands, feet, and sides. They say the blood that bled smelled of roses. This went on for fifty years until his death.

"Pray, hope and don't worry," was his wisdom to all.

Ask for his assistance, if you wish to have a deeper spiritual connection when you pray to him.

Your Guardian Angel

■ ■ ■

EVERYONE IS BORN WITH AT least two guardian angels from the time you are born until the time your cross over and through your transition. Their sole purpose is to assist you throughout your life.

They can only help you if you ask for their help. Why? Because if they intervene to assist you when you haven't asked them to, they would be treading on your "Free Will." The only time your guardian angel can intervene into your life is if you are in a do or die situation and it's not your time to go yet; in which case, they will save you.

As we grow older in our life, there are times when we have more than two angels around us, depending on what circumstances or challenges are going on in our lives. Certain angels have stronger abilities than others, according to the blessings or challenges you may be facing. The bottom line is just know you always have your personal guardian angels with you at all time to serve you. Just ask for their help and they will be there to serve you or give you the answer you are looking for.

As the saying goes, "Ask and you shall receive."

Archangel Ariel

■ ■ ■

"The lion and the lioness of God"

ARIEL IS REGARDED AS BOTH male and female spirit.

She is the protector of earth and all animals. When healing of injured animals is involved, she works closely with Archangel Raphael.

Call upon Archangel Ariel to manifest your dreams into your physical reality.

He will bless and purify your home.

Archangel Azrael

■ ■ ■

"He who helps God"

ARCHANGEL AZRAEL IS THE ANGEL that transitions us through death. He helps us through, as well as when we have crossed over.

He heals our hearts and souls to help us overcome the loss of our loved ones.

If you feel blocked in your personal life, call upon him to guide your way.

Angel Camael

■ ■ ■

"Divine Justice"

HE PROTECTS AND BRINGS PEACE to the world.

Angel Camael brings justice to all when dealing with karma.

Awareness of your inner holiness is brought to you through him.

Camael creates a balance to negate stress.

He helps to teach us self-discipline.

Archangel Chamuel

■ ■ ■

"He who seeks God"

HE IS UTTER LOVE.

He brings peace and protection to the world.

Chamuel helps our awareness to love thy self.

When dealing with depression, he helps you heal.

He brings balance to your life.

Archangel Chamuel gives power to those who need to learn the act of forgiveness, whether it is to forgive yourself or another.

Archangel Gabriel

■ ■ ■

"God is Mighty"

GABRIEL IS MOST KNOWN AS the messenger sent to the "Virgin Mary" to inform her she was with child, "the son of God." *

He brings security and protection during the times of any concerns while being pregnant.

Archangel Gabriel can help you manifest your deepest desires; however, his answers may not be immediate. You will always receive the answer at the most perfect or important time of your life, and when the timing is most profound.

When cleansing of mind, body, spirit and home is needed, call upon him.

While traveling, he protects you through violent weather.

He feeds your mind with great inspiration when you are feeling creative.

Gabriel's presence is strongly known when you see the streams of moonlight shining.

*We are all God's sons and daughters.

Archangel Gadiel

■ ■ ■

"God is my wealth"

GADIEL IS ASSOCIATED WITH THE wind you may feel his energy is at its peak when you feel the wind upon you. Or you can close your eyes and imagine yourself gracefully gliding through the sky, allowing the wind to support your body and soul to let go of all fears and worries.

He will keep your spirits up.

He builds your confidence when you are down and out.

He helps your work performance.

He will help fix a relationship that isn't going well.

Archangel Gadiel's love is so powerful and unconditional that he will help you release any negative feelings after dealing with any confrontation or strong disagreements.

He is capable of warding off all evil energy.

Archangel Haniel

■ ■ ■

"Grace of God"

SHE IS THE CAREGIVER ON earth and her gift to the world is to help others.

Archangel Haniel, when you call upon her, her love and wisdom will create harmony and balance for you and all human mankind.

Joy of material things is fleeting and true happiness is from within, which never leaves us. She prompts us to remember this.

Haniel helps us to make new friends.

She makes artistic abilities better.

One of her greatest blessings is to create balance in your life when you ask.

Archangel Metatron

■ ■ ■

"The one who sits next to God"

ARCHANGEL METATRON WAS THE ONLY Archangel that God transformed from being human to an angel.

The Akashic records, which are all the records of our deeds, good or bad, on earth as well as in heaven, are kept by him.

He guards the Tree of Life.

Metatron gives us knowledge to realize our potential as human beings.

He eases your grief.

He helps you connect with your higher self.

He is the Patron Angel of children.

Archangel Michael

■ ■ ■

"He who is like God"

MICHAEL IS THE LEADER OF all angels.

He is the Saint of law enforcement. His primary concern is protection, integrity, courage and strength.

When it comes to love, hope, and faith, he is the angel of deliverance.

He is the angel who protects "all" from lower and negative energies.

Call upon Archangel Michael to help you find your life's purpose.

Archangel Raziel

■ ■ ■

"Secrets of God"

WHEN GIVEN PERMISSION FROM GOD, Raziel reveals secrets of God.

Ask Raziel how to tap into the universe to gain spiritual guidance, so you may receive your deepest desires when knowing how to work the powerful love and energy that lies within all of us.

He is the patron of wisdom and knowledge who stands between heaven and earth.

He helps release any self-limited beliefs and behaviors.

With your open heart and mind, he will connect to your inner wisdom and spirit to help you manifest miracles as you ask.

He inspires original and wonderful ideas for you.

Need a new place to live or a new job? Call upon Raziel.

Archangel Uriel

■ ■ ■

"Force of God"

HE IS CAPABLE OF TRANSFORMING your worst nightmare into your biggest blessing.

He is the teacher of wisdom throughout your life's journey.

As we seek the answers of our spirituality, he provides us with strength and compassion to help us reach within for peace and understanding of oneself.

Archangel Zerachiel

■ ■ ■

"Command of God"

He will help you free yourself of addictions.

Parents that have addictions can count on him to watch over and protect their children. He gives them comfort as he wraps his wings around them.

A lost or ill pet; call upon Archangel Zerachiel for his assistance.

Zerachiel will help you sleep better.

When it comes to dealing with situations in life, there is saying
"It's all Good in the End!"
And if it's not good,
then it's not the end.

"Your Thoughts, Dreams and Prayers"

"Your Thoughts, Dreams and Prayers"

"Your Thoughts, Dreams and Prayers"

I highly recommend a book called Encyclopedia of Angels, Spirit Guides and Ascended Masters written by Susan Gregg, if you wish to know the deep meaning of all Angels, Saints and Ascended Masters.

Made in the USA
Columbia, SC
04 October 2018